The Collection 2017

compiled by John Field
foreword by Carol Klein

EXPRESS NEWSPAPERS

hamlyn

An Hachette UK Company
www.hachette.co.uk

First published in Great Britain in 2016 by Hamlyn,
a division of Octopus Publishing Group Ltd, Carmelite House,
50 Victoria Embankment, London EC4Y 0DZ
www.octopusbooks.co.uk

British Cartoon Archive

Cartoons supplied by British Cartoon Archive
Cartoons compiled by John Field
Page 3 photograph Express Newspapers
Page 89 note reproduced with permission of Robert Williams
Page 160 photograph Brian Gibbs/Alamy

ISBN 978 0 60062 955 9

A CIP catalogue record for this book is available from the British Library.

Printed and bound in China

10 9 8 7 6 5 4 3 2 1

Contents

Foreword

Carol Klein

It is a great honour to write the foreword to this year's *Giles: The Collection*, especially as it focuses on Grandma.

She is the enduring stalwart of the whole series and the one character, constant and recognisable, that everybody thinks of when they think of Giles's cartoons.

She is such a bundle of contradictions that readers can project their own take on a changing and confusing world onto her. But *she* is never confused, always adamant, acting without inhibition and convinced she's right. As a creation of Carl Giles's imagination, she reflects not his embarrassed alter ego but his unchecked id, shooting from the hip, saying whatever she pleases to whomever, regardless of rank or circumstance – an opinionated, anti-authoritarian, drinking, gambling, racketeering opportunist, pro-Soviet royalist.

Sitting in her chair, she looks like one of those dark sea anemones, black and amorphous, with a wrinkled upper lip, that, despite its overall immobility, might expand and snap you up at a moment's notice. She's even more terrifying on the move, raised umbrella in hand.

Most of the cartoons depict the chaotic aftermath of something she has just said – she very rarely actually speaks (the secret of her success). But above all, she is the centre of the family, around which assorted toddlers and pets revolve – all drawn with great detail and affection by Giles.

Visually, she is the 'black hole' in the cartoons, but, emotionally, she is the centre, not because of the family's indulgence, but because of her strength of character. She embodies a very British contrariness, and celebrates sheer bloody mindedness, not just on principle, but by habit.

My father took *The Express* and so, by default, my mother did, too. My parents ran a TV shop and there are so many TV set references in Giles, it sometimes feels as though his cartoons have special significance for me and my family. Each morning my mum would pick up the newspaper from the mat and plonk it on the breakfast table, leaving my dad to have a leisurely read before pottering in to work. She had already made everyone's breakfast, often put a stew in the oven for dinner (lunch to you) and got us ready for school, set the fire for later, fetched some coal before dashing to open the shop but before she did, on Giles days – three days a week – she always took a sneak preview of the cartoon. It was something to look forward to, but it was Grandma's antics that were the most endearing and made her giggle.

I suppose I've grown up with Giles. The Giles family and I both appeared within a few weeks of each other, though Grandma made her first appearance five years later. By then I'd just started school, while she appeared like Aphrodite, fully formed, ageless, timeless and immortal.

My grandmas were nothing like Giles's Grandma though. I suspect that, like she did for so many other people, she became the third grandma we all wished we'd had and, come to that, the character we all wish we could be, shameless yet blameless, a law unto herself.

I can't help wondering what stance she would have taken on Europe. Brexit or Bremain? Immediately, you assume Brexit, but Grandma is nothing if not a pragmatist – whatever suits her on the day. Double standards? Hypocrisy? No, just that same mixture of contradictions that personifies being British.

Carol Klein

Introduction: Grandma

The year 2016 saw the Centenary of Giles's birth (29 September 1916). In addition, the previous year witnessed the 70th anniversary of the first appearance of his Giles cartoon family. This year's collection focuses on Grandma, the most loved member of the family, as a tribute to Giles. He frequently used Grandma as a way of commenting on the ups and downs of life in the UK over a period of around half a century and it seems fitting to use her to mark the 100th anniversary of his birth.

From 1942 onwards, Giles lived in and around Ipswich and the town marked its strong links with the cartoonist a few years ago by renaming a main space, which was overlooked for many years by his studio, Giles Circus. The space is graced with a statue of Grandma and a few other members of the Giles cartoon family. Grandma is, of course, the main figure in the group and her presence dominates the whole space (see page 160).

The need for Grandma and the Giles family
With the end of World War II, Giles, a war correspondent at that time, obviously lost his main source of events and portfolio of characters (Hitler, Mussolini, etc.), on which he could base his cartoons. The first hint of the Giles family came from the Tommy in the 1945 cartoon (see page 31), who expresses the worries which Giles must have felt at the time. A short time after the war's end however, Giles hit upon the idea of creating a cartoon family as a vehicle for conveying many of his thoughts and comments, sometimes caustic, on national and world events. Consequently, in a cartoon dated 5 August 1945 (see page 32) Grandma, along with the whole Giles family, first appeared, just three months after the ending of the war in Europe.

Who was Grandma based upon?
Over time, there has been some debate about who Grandma was based upon. Some people suggest it was an amalgam of Giles's own two grandmothers, others have suggested that there is a resemblance with his boss at Express Papers, Lord Beaverbrook. To my mind, there is little doubt that her appearance is based upon Giles himself and his note to a friend (see page 89), on a cartoon showing the interior of a pub close to his farm in Suffolk seems to confirm as much. The cartoon was given by Giles to the publican in the cartoon, with a rather revealing note. See also the photograph of Giles and his drawing of Grandma on the Contents page – I do believe that we can assume that Grandma's character is based a little upon Giles himself and perhaps he used her to express some of his own views on certain events. The irascible nature of Grandma obviously struck a chord with the British people – she quickly became a firm favourite and Giles often used her as a mouthpiece for his comments on the world. Her insight into some world events, her views on life in the UK and thoughts on some decisions taken by those in power seemed to strike a chord with many people in this country.

Grandma and her football team
Like Giles himself, Grandma was an avid supporter of Ipswich Town Football Club. Unsurprisingly, he used Grandma as a means of celebrating the club winning the FA Cup Final in 1978. In a cartoon of her going up to Wembley (see cartoon dated 5 May 1978, page 62), he shows her leaving home on the morning of the match, leaving little doubt about who she was supporting.

Royalty

Grandma manages somehow to have a great admiration for the Soviet leaders such as Lenin, Kosygin and Gorbachev at the same time as being an ardent supporter of the Monarchy.

In his book, *The Giles Family*, Peter Tory tells us that the royal family enjoyed Giles's portraits of them in a number of cartoons, and, in total, own over 30 originals. Their high regard for Giles and his work was illustrated by the fact that when Prince Charles and Princess Anne were asked to organise a dinner to celebrate their parents' Silver Wedding, they asked Giles to illustrate the front cover of the menu, included here (see right). It will be seen that Giles decided to use his most famous cartoon character, Grandma, as a means for conveying the humour. An example of how, on occasions, Giles would link two cartoons sometimes years apart, is illustrated by the cartoon dated 20 April 1976 (see page 136), which refers back to the Silver Wedding menu card, over three years earlier.

Grandma's Sisters

In the introduction to the 2015 collection I explained that Grandma had two sisters up north, another in Aberdeen and a fourth somewhere near Aberystwyth. I warned then that this may not be all of them. I have since discovered, again in Peter Tory's book, reference to another sister in Ireland. Giles himself told Tory that "She turned up after one of our visits to Ireland. She was very like the South of England Grandma. She looked exactly like her and in fact the Manchester sisters – but in terms of Guinness she could probably drink them all under the table". I have been unable to find evidence of this latest sister in any cartoon, but I suspect that she is more than just an ugly rumour. I no longer feel able to suggest that this completes the set – particularly in the light of the following.

In cartoon dated 30 December 1969 (see page 15), it will be seen that, in addition to a photograph of a rather severe looking elderly woman entitled "Mummy", there is another photograph called "Albert, Botany Bay" – no doubt Grandma's father – in prison garb. It is interesting to note that she named her son after his grandfather. One also worries, therefore, whether, somewhere out in Australia, there is yet another Grandma sister or even sisters.

Addendum (Grandma's Sisters)

Unfortunately, I feel obliged to report that, whilst proofreading this Collection, I came across a reference to yet another sister, named Ivy, living somewhere near Grandma (see page 128). This makes a total of six sisters in the UK and Ireland, with possibly an unknown number in the Antipodes.

Although Grandma's idiosyncratic and complicated nature defies precise categorisation, I have attempted in this collection to capture some of her diverse contradictory character under the following ten headings:

Chapter 1   Grandma at Home

Grandma is possibly at her worst when at home because, as illustrated in this chapter, she is frequently at the centre of family activities and usually has a contrary opinion or caustic comment to expound about most events taking place in this chaotic household. She feels able, in this familiar environment which she usually attempts to totally control, to both chastise the children and to make life equally uncomfortable for the older members of the family with impunity. The amazing thing is that she gets away with her tyrannical behaviour almost completely and the only dissent from the rest of the family is usually made behind her back or out of earshot although, occasionally, the children seem able to put up an element of resistance.

Chapter 2   Grandma at Large

Outside the house, Grandma's behaviour is hardly any better than when indoors. She still feels that she has an unalienable right to express forceful views on a wide range of subjects without any thought of their impact on other people or the damage they may do. She is rarely able to take a joke if she is the butt of the humour but is unable to resist any opportunity to point out other peoples' shortcomings and make fun of them. She is unfazed by her surroundings, whether it is her banker's private office or at an important social occasion and takes her unassailable obstinacy and forthright views with her throughout her travels.

Chapter 3   Grandma's Sports and Hobbies

Unlikely as it may seem and despite her age, Grandma obviously still has a keen interest in a number of sports, both indoors and outside. Her golf swing, her total commitment to her local football team and horse racing generally, and her obvious prowess with a table tennis bat are some of the indications of a lively interest in sporting activities. The impressive display of acute agility, albeit as a result of an obviously painful injury during a game of beach cricket, shows that a great deal of life is still left beneath that rather ancient exterior. Her hobbies are equally revealing, from the enthusiastic leading, with a clarinet, of a children's musical recital in the house, to the despair of the rest of the family, through to the intellectual demands of a tough game of chess against one of her greatest rivals within the family pecking order, her grandson Ernie.

Chapter 4   Grandma the Gambler

Grandma is an inveterate gambler, particularly on the horses. However, she does not restrict herself simply to the races but is prepared to take a gamble on many things and is not averse to winning money from her grandchildren playing cards and even trying to charge Capital Gains Tax on her winnings from them. Even when waiting to see the doctor, she persuades the other patients to join in a game of bingo which she seems to be finding financially lucrative.

Chapter 5   Grandma at the Pub

Not a great surprise to most of us, Grandma can on occasions, be found enjoying a drink and a cigarette and, if possible, a little gossip in the local pub. Her tipple seems to range from a pint of beer or a bottle of stout or Guinness, sometimes with a whisky chaser, to white wine when being paid for by a visiting group of Cossacks. The general impression given is that she is able to take her drink well and it should be noted that, when at home, a bottle of beer is often within her reach along with a packet of cigarettes – even when she is in bed.

Chapter 6   Grandma at Church
It seems that Grandma's main consideration on her visits to church is to avoid giving actual money to the collection. On the occasions when she does give something, it is either a mistake or is relatively worthless. Sometimes she uses the visit to give the minister a piece of her mind or to offer him advice – not always well received.

Chapter 7   Grandma and the Health Service
Although Grandma usually seems happily at home in the doctors' waiting rooms, the doctors themselves appear to be less pleased to see her there – probably with good reason. When it comes to hospitals, however, Grandma tends to be more her normal grumpy self, making life difficult for those hospital staff unfortunate enough to find themselves having to deal with her. Her charm offensive regarding the Health Service is extensive enough to include chemist shops and even veterinary surgeons.

Chapter 8   Grandma and the Law
Grandma's inherent dislike of the law and all those who work to uphold it is a fundamental element of her character. The only time she seems to see its value is when she decides to preside over a kangaroo court, held at home, to hear a case involving the unlawful swigging of a bottle of stout, alleged to be in the ownership of Grandma, by one of the younger members of the family. However, it has to be noted that on one occasion she actually came to the rescue of a police officer in the mistaken belief that he was under attack – her sense of duty prevailed for once, perhaps.

Chapter 9   Grandma the Royalist and Political Activist
One of the many contradictions we find with Grandma is the bewildering conflict between her views regarding the monarchy and her obvious support for the communist regime of the former USSR (seeking to welcome first Kosygin and then Gorbachev) to the UK. To most people these views would seem to be mutually exclusive and it is hard to see how she can sustain an extreme sense of loyalty to our dynastic system while, at the same time, taking great pains to personally welcome Soviet leaders to this country. However, Grandma manages to pull off this feat with aplomb and without any personal sense of contradiction. Her other involvements with politics also show strong inconsistency with a wide range of political issues.

Chapter 10   Grandma and Anger Management
Anger management is something which Grandma has taken to heart and this chapter illustrates how successful she has been in channeling her natural tendency to see red, given a degree of provocation, to the maximum benefit. When in a state of fury, Grandma's vigorous reactions ignore her victim's status or her surroundings. The fact that she is chastising an officer of a famous sailing club or feels badly dealt with by the judges at the Chelsea Flower Show, does not inhibit the ardour of her attack. It is possible that this element of her character has strengthened with age.

I hope that readers will get as much pleasure out of this exposé of a nationally important figure as I have had compiling it.

John Field

Grandma at Home

After two years of planning, Billy Graham, a young American evangelist, had begun his Greater London Crusade. It was the biggest single venture in evangelism attempted at that time, with a total of 1,750,000 attending the crusade during its twelve-week period and, long before the end, its impact was being felt throughout the country.

"Mr. Billy Graham has told America that one in four first-born Britons are born out of wedlock, so Grandma insists that we find her birth certificate."

Daily Express, 18 March 1954

"Decorations are an essential part of the gaiety of Christmas ... the whole family is drawn closer together by the fragile links of a paper chain." – *Daily Express* yesterday.

Daily Express, 13 December 1956

With ever increasing travel by air, the Aircraft Noise Bill, 1966 was introduced two days before this cartoon appeared. Its primary intention was to restrain nuisance by aircraft noise.

"It would have to be a handy-sized aircraft to make enough noise to get through to this house."

Daily Express, 28 July 1966

"They're signing a two-day truce with Grandma. They won't play any Christmas jokes on her if she promises she won't sing."

Daily Express, 24 December 1968

14 To the great surprise of the American public, President Nixon had ordered the US to stop any further work on the development of its biological weapons programme. He renounced any first use by the US of chemical weapons designed to incapacitate as well as those that kill.

"Pity. Vera's thrived on it all her life."

Daily Express, 27 November 1969

This was a period which saw the spread of "Hong Kong Flu" around the world. Obviously the children were taking no chances with their new pet. Note the pictures, including Albert (Grandma's father?) – enjoying a holiday in Australia, her mother, her cousin Norris (who obviously came to a sticky end), and one of her political heroes.

"Don't fly off the handle, Grandma – we're only using your bed while our Christmas present's got flu."

Daily Express, 30 December 1969

Another picture of Albert!

"This is the same one as you gave me last year – I wrote the 1969 Grand National odds on the bottom."

Sunday Express, 8 March 1970

The day before, a health expert had informed a meeting of the British Veterinary Association that "Pet owning could be as dangerous as living with a time bomb". He added that pets could carry the "silent danger" of many kinds of deadly infections.

"I think you're as safe kissing Butch as you know who."

Daily Express, 17 September 1970

Note Butch the dog cowering under the table – is that Rupert Bear, without his jacket, in his mouth?
(See page 34).

"Who's been having a go at the bottle of whisky we bought dad for Father's Day?"

Sunday Express, 20 June 1971

Since its inception in 1954, *Sports Illustrated*, an American sports magazine, annually presented the Sportsman of the Year award to "the athlete or team whose performance that year most embodies the spirit of sportsmanship and achievement". Both Americans and non-Americans are eligible. The first award was made to British athlete Roger Bannister for "track and field" events, having run the first sub 4-minute mile earlier that year. In 1999, the magazine began to use "Sportswoman" or "Sportswomen" in appropriate cases.

"She'll give you 'Sportsman of the Year' if you miss."

Daily Express, 14 November 1972

20 Dr. Timothy Jay, a psychologist at the Massachusetts College of Liberal Arts had explained that swearing "allows us to vent or express anger, joy, surprise, happiness". He added, "cursing is more than just aggression – it's like the horn on your car, you can do a lot of things with that, it's built into you."

"As a matter of fact I did read that a doctors' journal said that swearing is good for you – but not that good."

Sunday Express, 14 April 1974

"They're voting what to call Grandma after the Sex Discrimination Act begins tomorrow – 'Jaws' or 'Sir'."

Sunday Express, 28 December 1975

22   The period between November, 1975 and June, 1976 was called the "Third Cod War". Iceland had claimed that the ocean up to 200 nautical miles (370 km) from its coast fell under its authority. The British government did not accept this large extension to Icelandic control, and as a result, British fishermen continued to fish in the disputed area. A major incident occurred just before the appearance of this cartoon, when HMS Andromeda collided with an Icelandic vessel. The British Ministry of Defence said that the collision was a "deliberate attack" on the British warship "without regard for life", whilst the Icelanders said that Andromeda had rammed their vessel by "overtaking the boat and then swiftly changing course".

"Grandma, with a grave international crisis over the future of cod you're not supposed to give yours to the cat."

Daily Express, 26 January 1976

After the 1981 inner-city riots, the personal approval ratings of Margaret Thatcher, the Prime Minister, dropped. At the time, Australian George Negus, in a "60 Minutes" TV interview, asked her about some people saying that, on occasions, she was "plain pig-headed and won't be told by anybody" which caused a certain amount of comment in the national press.

"When it comes to stubborn, pig-headed iron ladies – we've got our built-in model T."

Sunday Express, 18 October 1981

24 At this time, the annual licence for colour TV had just gone up to £46 from £34, which it had been since November 1979.

"Grandma – stop saying over and over 'I'm not paying £46 for that!' YOU don't pay anything for that."

Daily Express, 3 December 1981

In January, 1982, there was a period of 24-hour strikes about plans by British Rail management to implement flexible rosters which would mean footplate staff working a variable length day, causing considerable disruption to the travelling public. Ray Buckton, the leader of the Associated Society of Locomotive Engineers and Firemen at the time, received death threats, and "unsightly items" were pushed through his letterbox. Sir Peter Parker was Chairman of the British Railways Board during this period. Presumably, Grandma's important travelling plans had been upset.

"The Valentines Grandma sent to Ray Buckton and Sir Peter Parker – they're charging her for sending obscene literature through the post."

Sunday Express, 14 February 1982

Four days after this cartoon appeared, a debate in the House of Commons was programmed to discuss Law and Order issues, including hanging.

"Here come three of my good reasons for bringing back hanging."

Sunday Express, 21 March 1982

The "Hitler Diaries" were purchased as authentic by the West German magazine *Stern*. However, subsequent forensic examination proved that they were fakes. Maybe Ernie had a point.

"I didn't SAY she wrote them – I only said she COULD have written them."

Daily Express, 26 April 1983

Four days earlier, after a long period with the country snowed under with some of the coldest weather on record, the newspapers reported that the Government bowed to pressure and agreed to make a £5 cold weather payment to needy pensioners everywhere – as reports poured in of "elderly people dying miserable deaths alone in their freezing homes".

"Grandma's making sure she gets her extra £5 worth."

Sunday Express, 18 January 1987

This cartoon may not be completely accurate. The Guinness World Records indicate that, in fact, a lady named as Dorothy had left £2.5 million to animal charities. However, it also states that her brother, Ben, who died a few days after her, had left £7 million to his cat "Blackie".

"You're wasting your time, cat – the most she'll leave you is her lucky charm and half a bottle of peppermints."

Daily Express, 12 May 1988

The Government did discuss this idea at the time but it did not go ahead, being considered "unworkable".

"If we're all going to have Identity Cards, grandma can use the same one she had in 1939."

Daily Express, 27 September 1988

Grandma at Large

The Tommy was probably expressing thoughts which were passing through Giles's head at the time. This concern almost certainly resulted in the birth of Grandma and the rest of the Giles family – see the next cartoon.

"Musso gorn, Goering gorn – you'll be in the cart when they've all gorn – won't 'ave nuffin to draw, will you?"

Daily Express, January 1945

The first appearance of the Giles family, with a grumpy-looking Grandma at the rear. This shows a length of railway line close to Giles's farm on the outskirts of Ipswich.

It's quicker by rail.

Sunday Express, 5 August 1945

"Lady, don't ask me why they always have to have pictures of pretty girls to sell their cars – just go eat your sausage roll somewhere else."

Daily Express, 18 October 1962

34　At the time a national price war was raging regarding cigarettes. Note, near the window, the tiny figure of Rupert Bear, the Giles family's big rival at the *Daily Express*, dangling by a noose (the other dolls are safely secured on the shelf). This is not the only occasion in his cartoons when Giles expressed similar thoughts regarding Rupert, whom he presumably considered was a major competitor for the affection of the *Express* newspapers' readers.

"That one makes me nervous. If she's still paying me full price for her cigarettes she must be having me on something else."

Daily Express, 17 January 1967

The day before, the US Government, keen to defend the dollar at a difficult time, requested that the London Gold Market should close for a day. The result was a buying stampede which, it is recorded, shattered all previous records. Grandma was obviously an avid follower of the precious metals market.

"Inform Madam the marking on her valuable heirloom does not read 22 carat. It reads 'A present from Blackpool made in Germany.'"

Sunday Express, 17 March 1968

This was a period of concern about the likelihood of a banking crisis with increasing loss of investor confidence. Obviously Grandma was taking no risks.

"Lack of confidence in the management has compelled Madam to adopt panic measures and withdraw her entire account – i.e. £4 7s. 3d."

Daily Express, 24 February 1970

"I'm not hijacking her – just a little trap to stop her nicking my marrows for this year's Harvest Festival."

Sunday Express, 13 September 1970

The impending decimalisation of the UK currency was causing considerable unrest amongst some people in the country – as illustrated by Grandma's shrewd calculations here.

"According to her new decimal prices, the mints work out at 11s. 6d. each and 9d extra for the holes."

Daily Express, 9 February 1971

In mid-November of this year, the "Series D" pictorial £5 note was issued. Three days before this cartoon appeared, police in Amsterdam, Holland had detained three Englishmen in connection with the discovery of £100,000 worth of £5 notes – Giles had exaggerated the situation a little on the newspaper poster.

"I'll tell you why we're suspicious – because this is the fifth fiver you've changed this morning for a penny oxo cube."

Sunday Express, 28 November 1971

Grandma being Grandma! Note that her son must have been a worker at the newspaper offices.

"There's always one – says she's taken the paper for 50 years and she wants her money back."

Daily Express, 17 March 1977

The song, "There's No One Quite Like Grandma", by the primary school choir from St. Winifred's School in Stockport was number-one in the UK Singles Chart from 27 December 1980 to 3 January 1981.

"Lady, you've played it 93 times – are you going to buy the bloody thing or not?"

Daily Express, 18 December 1980

At this time, a London-wide bus strike was taking place.

"I don't think madam appreciated your little joke, offering her a broom as alternative transport."

Daily Express, 29 June 1982

The Government was discussing the future Admiralty Jurisdiction Regulations Act, which referred to the laws relating to salvage 43 of shipping. This cartoon is a good example of Giles giving a rather obscure reference to a national issue and, of course, he was a keen yachtsman, being President of Felixstowe Ferry Sailing Club, located just a few miles from his farm.

"Madam, because there happens to be nobody aboard, it does not mean this ship is abandoned, and what you have there is not salvage – it's loot!"

Daily Express, 6 January 1983

44 A major miners' strike, relating to pit closures, began in March, 1984 and did not end until the following year. The leak referred to in the cartoon relates to possible secret discussions taking place at a high level at that time about even further pit closures.

"Your wish to withdraw your account because of the Thatcher bank leak causes us great concern, especially as I see you are £3.50 in the red."

Daily Express, 8 March 1984

The Bank of England £1 note was first issued in 1797 but, following the introduction on 21 April, 1983 of the £1 coin, it was withdrawn from circulation on 11 March 1988. The shopkeeper obviously knew Grandma well.

"I know she's not likely to carry many 50 pound notes – but with her we check the pounds."

Daily Express, 24 April 1984

Six days earlier, the Food Group Meat Panel had issued a report, which appeared in the *Journal of the Science of Food and Agriculture*, relating to meat levels in various processed foods.

"She wants them all cut up for examination – who wrote that article about the public not getting enough meat in their bangers?"

Daily Express, 12 March 1985

This relates to celebrations for the 40th anniversary of the ending of the War in Europe. Of course, the war in the Far East continued for more than another three months.

"I remember letting her have extra food rations for the Victory Street Party in 1945 – and we all know where they finished up."

Daily Express, 7 May 1985

Two days earlier, 150 rival English football fans battled with knives and broken bottles aboard a North Sea ferry in a fierce brawl which left four people seriously injured.

"We don't often get punch-ups on this ferry – unless somebody refuses to vacate this lady's favourite seat right now."

Sunday Express, 10 August 1986

The Duchess of Windsor had just put up for sale, at auction in London, a range of jewels given to her by the former King Edward VIII including eleven pieces by Cartier, which sold for £8 million.

"Not quite in the Duchess of Windsor bracket – I'll give you £1.50 for the lot."

Sunday Express, 5 April 1987

"You tell me once more you expect I was at their opening ceremony and you'll be needing them."

Sunday Express, 21 June 1987

Comedian Lenny Henry and the comedy scriptwriter Richard Curtis, founded the charity, Comic Relief, in 1985 in response to the famine in Ethiopia. An important part of the money raising effort today is Red Nose Day, which was first introduced at the time this cartoon appeared.

"You asked for that – 'Funny comic nose, Madam? Oh, I see you've already got one!"

Daily Express, 2 February 1988

At this time, the Convention on International Trade in Endangered Species of Wild Fauna and Flora (CITES) banned the international trade in ivory.

"I bet she didn't know her umbrella handle was made of ivory"

Sunday Express, 4 June 1989

Grandma's Sports and Hobbies

The season for red deer stags in England, Northern Ireland and Wales is from 1 August until 30 April; in Scotland it is from 1 July until 20 October.

"Madam! How dare you wear a fox fur during the stag hunting season?"

Daily Express, 4 September 1951

54

This relates to the 1960 Wimbledon Ladies Singles semi-final, which Christine Truman lost to Maria Bueno of Brazil (6-0, 5-7, 6-1).

"How many of you playing this Christine Truman match this afternoon?"

Daily Express, 30 June 1960

The Women's pole vault event was not introduced into the Olympic Games until 2000, so Grandma's practicing was 40 years too early.

"Grandma! For heaven's sake forget there's a grandma competing in the Olympic Games –
you're too late for the selectors, anyway."

Daily Express, 18 August 1960

This relates to the 1962 British Open Championship, the oldest of the four major championships in professional golf held in the United Kingdom. It was played at Troon Golf Club in Scotland and was won by Arnold Palmer.

"What's he glaring at me for? I said 'Pardon'."

Daily Express, 10 July 1962

The weather between September, 1964 and May, 1965 was particularly bad with a considerable amount of snow lying around for long periods.

"On the other hand there's nothing in the rules to say skis CAN'T be worn"

Daily Express, 2 March 1965

The Grand National Horse Race at Aintree Racecourse took place the day before.

"Watch out for the wild swings to the body, the swift uppercuts – her horse fell at the first fence and her team got knocked out of the semi-finals."

Sunday Express, 28 March 1965

This relates to the World Chess Championship, 1972, between the defending champion, Boris Spassky of the then Soviet Union, and the challenger, Bobby Fischer, of the United States. It took place in Reykjavík, Iceland and had been called the Match of the Century. Fischer's behaviour, at the time, was full of contradictions and he failed to arrive for the opening ceremony on July 1st. He finally arrived in Iceland and agreed to play after a two-day postponement of the match.

"I'd like to see this Bobby Fischer try his tantrums here – when Grandma says 'Play' you play."

Daily Express, 6 July 1972

That wide swing was not really going to help Grandma's prowess with the croquet stick but, no doubt, it helped give vent to some of her anger.

"I tell you every year it's a waste of money buying your Mother flowers for Mother's Day."

Sunday Express, 24 March 1974

The first one-day cricket World Cup, organised by the International Cricket Conference, was held in England from 7–21 June 1975. Two days before this cartoon appeared, Australia had beaten Sri Lanka by 52 runs. In a semi-final, on 18 June, Australia beat England by 4 wickets but, 3 days later, lost the final by 17 runs to the West Indies.

"That's how the Aussies do it – bowl 'em on the feet, make 'em hop out of their crease, and BINGO!!"

Daily Express, 13 June 1975

There is no doubt which team Grandma supported. That afternoon, Ipswich beat Arsenal 1-0 at Wembley and the following morning's *Sunday Express* carried another cartoon with a jubilant Grandma returning home, accompanied by Butch the dog with the Cup in his mouth.

"I wouldn't be Bobby Robson if they lose, and I wouldn't be the Arsenal team if they win."

Daily Express, 5 May 1978

Alex Higgins, a Northern Irish professional snooker player, was nicknamed "Hurricane" because of his fast play.
The 1981 Masters snooker tournament took place from 27 January to 1 February at the Wembley Conference Centre.
Higgins won the tournament by beating Terry Griffiths 9-6.

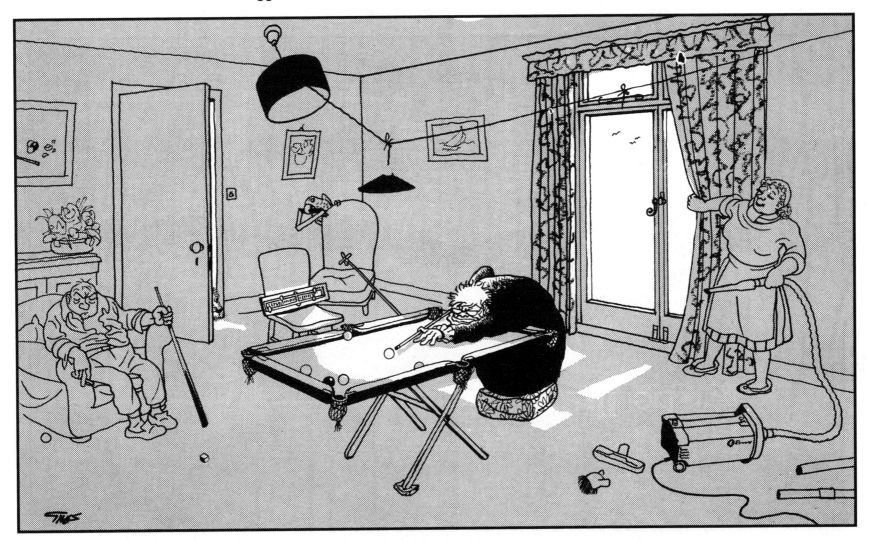

"Okay, Hurricane Higgins – Easter's over!"

Daily Express, 21 April 1981

64 Five months earlier, John McEnroe had defeated Björn Borg in the Gentlemen's Singles tennis final at the 1981 Wimbledon Championships. McEnroe's attitude on court during the 1981 tournament was controversial. He came close to being thrown out after he called umpire, Ted James, "the pits of the world" and then swore at tournament referee Fred Hoyles. He also made famous the phrase "you cannot be serious", by shouting it after several umpires' calls during his matches.

"You come a McEnroe with me and I'll maim yer."

Daily Express, 17 November 1981

"Then the accused said: 'How about a couple to take home for the wife?' Thereby committing an act of bribery and corruption."

Sunday Express, 25 July 1982

At this time, the ownership of the Aintree racecourse, near Liverpool, had changed from the Topham family to a property developer, Bill Davies, and there was considerable worry about the future of the course. Grandma was obviously part, in theory, of a nationwide campaign to save the Grand National course.

"What's the betting Aintree doesn't see a penny of it?"

Daily Express, 12 April 1983

Over the years, John McEnroe built up a reputation for bad behaviour on court. Two years earlier, playing in a tournament in Stockholm, McEnroe had a notorious outburst on court in which he called the umpire a "jerk". He was suspended for 21 days. The following year, he reached the singles final at the US Open but was beaten by Lendl. By 1986, the pressures of playing at the top had become too much and he took a six-month break and, therefore, missed that year's Wimbledon tournament. Returning to tennis later in 1986, he was again suspended in 1987 for two months and fined for misconduct and verbal abuse on court. It is dubious that Grandma had really intended to go Wimbledon in a true sporting spirit.

"If you're going to keep on about missing the punch-ups between McEnroe and the umpires, we're glad you're not coming."

Daily Express, 3 July 1986

Grandma the Gambler

Johnny Longden was an American jockey, born in Yorkshire, England. He was given the prestigious American George Woolf Memorial Jockey Award in 1952, which honours a rider "whose career and conduct exemplify the very best example of participants in the sport of thoroughbred racing". In fact, the race was won by American-bred, British-trained "Never say Die", ridden by an 18-year-old jockey, Lester Piggott, causing a sensation in the racing world.

"I for one ain't going to be around if Johnny Longden upsets your grandma's system."

Daily Express, 1 June 1954

At the time, some people felt that the Archbishop of Canterbury had snubbed Georgy Malenkov when, the previous Easter Sunday, the ex-Soviet Premier visited the Cathedral. It was reported that "the Russians were not saying but they were startled out of their usual composure when they stepped forward to speak to the Archbishop and he swept past them without a glance". Obviously Grandma was a shrewd gambler. The phone number above the door was that of an Ipswich bookmaker at that time and presumably Grandma visited the establishment on many occasions.

"Shilling each way Frisky Scot for the Lincolnshire and an even shilling Dr. Fisher doesn't ask Malenkov round for tea."

Sunday Express, 18 March 1956

"Anybody here ride the last horse in the last race?"

Daily Express, 22 March 1960

"While we may accept the Russians' claim that bingo is a grave illness we are not having sessions in my waiting-room while waiting for treatment."

Daily Express, 3 October 1961

Capital Gains Tax was first introduced 5 days before this cartoon appeared.

"Dad – is there any rule that we have to pay Grandma Capital Gains Tax on her winnings?"

Sunday Express, 11 April 1965

At the time, it was reported that "With teachers on strike, many parents wish they could fill the gap by teaching their own children". It was considered that "Provided there is a clear enough programme of work to follow, parents will do just as well as a nonexistent teacher". Obviously that view had not taken Grandma into account.

"Mum, are you sure Grandma's the right one to be carrying on their lessons while the teachers are on strike?"

Daily Express, 19 February 1970

74 A new Gaming Act introduced far greater restrictions on all gaming, including bingo and slot machines. From that date, they were subject to licence and placed under the control of the Gaming Board, which answered to the Home Office.

"She argues that we let 'em queue all night for Wimbledon or Covent Garden."

Daily Express, 30 June 1970

The previous day, Manchester United had beaten Liverpool 2–1 in the FA Cup Final at Wembley. All three goals came in a five-minute period early in the second half and United's victory prevented Liverpool from winning the treble of the League Title, the FA Cup and the European Cup.

"Know why I think this betting slip is a forgery? Because I can't remember giving anyone 500-1 against Manchester United and I don't spell Cup Final with a K."

Sunday Express, 22 May 1977

76 *Dallas* was a very popular TV programme and, at that time there was considerable national speculation about a murder attempt against one of the character in the show – J R Ewing. The popular interviewer, Terry Wogan, was frequently on television at that time but was not really thought to be implicated.

"Fiver Terry Wogan, because if he isn't on the Dallas show it's the only one he ain't."

Daily Express, 27 May 1980

In April, 1985, snooker became the first professional sport to introduce a drugs testing policy. Note that Rupert Bear is being used as a target by Stinker (see page 34).

"She's won me moneybox, piggy bank, half an Easter egg, me conkers and me knife – I reckon she's on dope!"

Daily Express, 11 April 1985

Grandma obviously considered that there was a good chance of the popular TV interviewer, Terry Wogan, taking over as Prime Minister of the country and a politician, Michael Heseltine, who had resigned his post as Secretary of State for Defence five days earlier, replacing an unpopular character in a TV soap opera at that time.

"What odds will we give her on Wogan to move into No. 10 and Heseltine to take over Dirty Den on TV?"

Daily Express, 14 January 1986

It had been announced that Irish singer, Bob Geldof, and British TV presenter Paula Yates, were to marry in Las Vegas after 10 years together. At the 1986 World Cup competition in Mexico, England had started badly, losing their first match against Portugal and drawing their second match against Morocco. The day before this cartoon appeared, their manager, Bobby Robson, had changed the team's tactics for their match against Poland and they won 3-0. However, they were knocked-out at the Quarter Finals stage, 10 days later, by Argentina winning 2-1 (including Maradona's "Hand of God" goal).

"Trust her to win both bets – right about Bob Geldof and right about Bobby Robson."

Daily Express, 12 June 1986

Grandma at the Pub

Giles's comments relate to an important conference being held in Geneva at that time, which considered the questions of the possible reunification of Germany, the Atlantic Pact and the achievement of enduring peace in the world.

"Aware that all jokes, articles, etc., should be about the Four-Power conference this week, I regret I cannot let the suggestion in yesterday's *Express* go by without comment. To 'check the fall-off in beer drinking, publicans should serve their beer on ice'."

Daily Express, 21 July 1955

The British Government had revealed that it suspected that considerable spy activity had been taking place at various trade shows and delegations, some involving museums and art historians. Giles obviously felt that information much more useful to the Russians could be found in the typical British pub.

Daily Express Comment: "In half an hour in a country pub the Russians would learn far more about the British than in all the museums and trading centres in the land." "I'll say they would."

Daily Express, 26 February 1963

82

There was considerable concern in Britain at the time about the United States military action in Vietnam, with massive demonstrations outside the US Embassy in London on the day this cartoon appeared. Maybe Grandma had sympathy with the demonstrators.

"Because you heard the lady say she supports President Johnson doesn't entitle you to go and hit her."

Sunday Express, 3 July 1966

Grandma and Alf Garnet, from the British TV sitcom *Til Death Us Do Part*, together in a pub, would be a strong cause for concern to any publican.

"And bang goes the Lounge trade."

Sunday Express, 18 February 1968

84 This was a period when Britain, along with many other Western countries, suffered substantial petroleum shortages and power cuts and lengthy blackouts became a fact of life. In December, 1970, some hospitals were forced to function on batteries and candles during a "work-to-rule" strike. Obviously some people were prepared to take advantage from this situation – including Grandma?

"Right – if I give you my solemn promise not to short-change you, have I got your word you won't underpay me?"

Daily Express, 8 December 1970

"She claims she rescued Winston Churchill when she was a WAAF in the Boer War."

Sunday Express, 9 November 1986

"They'll get hey nonny nonny if one of 'em lands on Grandma's foot."

Sunday Express, 3 May 1987

Michael Edwards, better known as Eddie "The Eagle", was a British skier who, in 1988, became the first competitor to represent Great Britain in ski jumping, at the Winter Olympics in Calgary, Canada. He finished last in both the 70 metres and 90 metres events.

"Our ski jumper is not the only one good at being last."

Sunday Express, 21 February 1988

Edwina Currie became a Junior Health Minister in 1986. Among her comments over the next two years were that old people who couldn't afford their heating bills should wrap up warm in winter and could avoid hypothermia by wearing "woolly hats and long johns".

"To avoid some grievous bodily harm get Grandma out by the back door before she sees who's just come in."

Sunday Express, 25 September 1988

This is in one of Giles's locals near his farm. The extract is from a copy of the cartoon, given to the publican behind the bar, with Giles's note giving a heavy hint that Grandma was, in fact, based upon himself.

(Any likeness to any living person purely coincidental.)

"These TV Soap boozers Princess Diana complains about –
we could do with a few round here."

Daily Express, 26 January 1989

Grandma at Church

This was a very severe winter – the snow started on the previous Boxing Day and the big freeze did not finish until March. The arctic conditions closed many schools, telephone lines were brought down and power cuts hit thousands of homes.

"Grandma, if you can't take your ice skates off stop stamping your feet to get warm"

Sunday Express, 27 January 1963

Green Shield stamps, introduced in 1958 and withdrawn in 1991, were a sales promotional scheme designed to reward shopping by providing gifts to customers.

"There go the last of grandma's green stamps."

Sunday Express, 8 December 1963

See also page 37.

"You didn't plough any fields and scatter – you nicked that marrow from my allotment on the way here."

Sunday Express, 2 October 1966

The third quarter of 1968 saw an improvement in the economic situation over the second, resulting in this change in the Bank Rate. Incidentally, it looks as if Grandma has managed to inveigle Vera in her regular Harvest Festival contribution scheme involving a stolen marrow.

"As the Bank Rate's been cut ½% may I suggest this week you put something in instead of whipping something out."

Sunday Express, 22 September 1968

The day before this cartoon appeared, the Post Office workers had supported the Overseas Telegraph operators in a pay dispute with a one-day strike.

"As Grandma had a three-draw win I've just said a little prayer for our postman in case the GPO didn't deliver her coupon."

Sunday Express, 2 February 1969

"My Grandma swallowed three holly berries in her cornflakes this morning."

Sunday Express, 23 December 1969

As I am sure Grandma could have told us, officially the Flat Season runs, in any year, from the day the Lincoln Handicap is programmed until the afternoon the November Handicap is run, or "such earlier or later dates as the British Horseracing Authority shall decide". The Lincoln Handicap is held at Doncaster racecourse in late March or early April, (usually taking place one or two weeks before the Grand National) and the November Handicap is also run at Doncaster and is scheduled to take place, each year, early in the month. The lesson chosen for that day obviously contravened all that Grandma held dear.

"What sort of lesson is THAT for the day before the opening of the flat?"

Sunday Express, 22 March 1970

This was a period of increasing fuel shortages, which culminated in Prime Minister Edward Heath announcing a number of measures two weeks after this cartoon appeared, commonly known as the "Three-Day Week". These measures included limiting industrial and commercial energy consumption to three consecutive days each week from the start of the New Year.

"Well there's one place where I bet they're not short of fuel."

Sunday Express, 2 December 1973

The day before, it was announced that 70 detectives would be keeping watch at the turnstiles at Wembley for thousands of "excellently printed" forged £1 Cup Final tickets.

"The Cup Final and Newmarket falling on the same day as our jumble sale was adversary enough, without a certain member of our congregation passing off forged raffle tickets."

Sunday Express, 5 May 1974

"I've had a word with the lady, Vicar. She's not collecting for the Church Restoration Fund, she's collecting for Grandma's Day."

Sunday Express, 20 October 1974

At this time, showers of sleet and snow occurred across most of Britain, particularly over the Easter period.

Seasonal Greetings

Daily Express, 29 March 1975

Ronnie Biggs, involved in the Great Train Robbery in 1963, escaped from Wandsworth Prison in 1965 where he was serving a 30-year sentence. Whilst living as a fugitive in Brazil, he was kidnapped by a gang of British ex-soldiers on 18 March 1981. Two days before this cartoon appeared, however, he was rescued from a yacht by Barbadian police.

"I thought you might have put up a prayer of thanksgiving for the salvation of poor Mr. Biggs."

Sunday Express, 26 April 1981

102 In March of the previous year, US President Ronald Reagan, in a speech to the National Association of Evangelicals, applied the phrase "evil empire" to the then Soviet Union. The following summer, 14 Eastern Bloc countries, led by the Soviet Union, boycotted the Summer Olympic Games being held in Los Angeles (possibly linked to the US-led boycott of the 1980 Summer Olympics in Moscow over the Soviet war in Afghanistan). The boycotted countries organized another major event, called the Friendship Games, also in the summer of 1984, in the Soviet Union.

"If he once mentions the Olympic Games or tells us we're all runners in the great race against evil, I'm withdrawing to the Spotted Cow."

Sunday Express, 5 August 1984

Grandma and the Health Service

In a parliamentary debate, the Minister of Health had stated that a shilling charge for prescriptions would save the Exchequer £12m. In response, Labour politician, Aneurin Bevan, referred to recent arbitration which had given doctors £10m a year, with £40m back pay, and stated that "the award had shocked the majority of people in Britain".

"If it wasn't for people like Vera we wouldn't want a health service."

Daily Express, 29 March 1952

The US sent a chimpanzee, named Ham, into space, 5 days earlier, as part of its space programme – he returned to earth alive and well. This coincided with an increase in National Health prescriptions in the UK. When the National Health Service was established in 1948, all prescriptions were free. Charges were introduced in 1952 at a rate of 1 shilling per prescription (irrespective of number of items involved) and in 1956 the rules were changed so that a charge applied to each item prescribed. In February 1961 it was doubled to 2 shillings per item. Grandma was obviously not too pleased.

"Madam, I haven't the faintest idea whether the extra charge for your cough mixture is going to be frittered away on some fool Government scheme to send monkeys to the moon."

Sunday Express, 5 February 1961

The General Secretary of the Medical Practitioners Union had stated that the recently announced financial provision for general medical services represented "a betrayal of the whole concept of the NHS which is clearly condemned to the status of a fourth-rate service". He considered that "an increase of £12m, or 2.5%, on the totally inadequate 1964 levels was unacceptable decay".

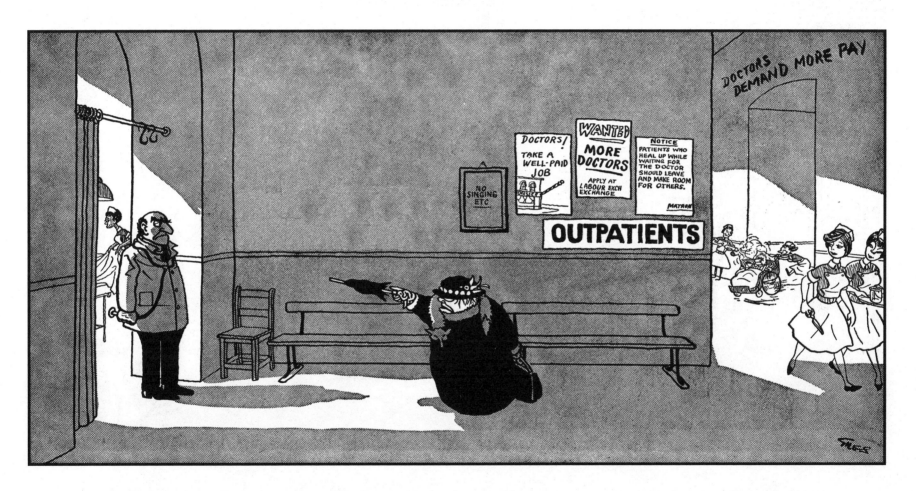

"If you say there's nothing wrong with me every time I come to see you then you're getting paid for nothing."

Daily Express, 1 October 1965

In Cape Town, two days earlier, Dr. Christiaan Barnard had performed the third heart transplant in the world on a 59-year-old man. The man survived the operation and lived for a further nineteen months.

"Watch 'im Vera – he'll have your heart out and shove it in Mrs. Harris before you can say Happy New Year."

Daily Express, 4 January 1968

In this week, doctors were awarded a pay increases averaging 30%. Regarding the weather, this doctor must have been lucky, as the Meteorological Office's report for April, 1975 states that "sunshine was below average for almost everywhere" but then added "there were some sunny days during the month – particularly during the last week when a number of places in Southern and South West England and the Channel Islands had prolonged sunny spells". Obviously he was not as lucky, however, in having Grandma as a patient.

"Doctor, you know you were saying how happy you are – all this extra money and fewer patients because the sun is shining?"

Daily Express, 25 April 1975

It was reported that doctors in hospitals in several parts of the country would only be treating emergency cases as part of an unofficial protest against new contracts, which could effectively cut the salaries of some of them.

"As you've been hanging around here for the last twenty years with your grumbling appendix I doubt if Doctor will classify you as an emergency."

Daily Express, 9 October 1975

It had been revealed that some family doctors had been recording patients' conversations in the privacy of their consulting room, without their knowledge or consent, to be used later as teaching aids.

"This recording of today's patients doesn't throw much light on their medical history, but it throws a lot of light on the form for the 3.30 at Newmarket."

Daily Express, 30 October 1975

At the general practitioners' annual meeting at Glasgow three days earlier, doctors demanded a 15% pay increase and threatened to take action which would cripple the National Health Service unless a satisfactory offer was made.

"For this one I want time and a half, danger money and a month in the Bahamas after each visit."

Daily Express, 22 July 1977

A doctor in Devon was struck off the Medical Register for "serious professional misconduct" after being found guilty of having intimate relations with three women patients. He had used hypnotism, love fantasies and drug cocktails to seduce them.

"Watch 'im Vera"

Daily Express, 25 November 1982

112   In Canterbury, a consultant surgeon had resigned after it was revealed that he had allowed a veterinary surgeon to assist him in a routine hernia operation. The vet was allowed to help at the beginning and end of the operation. It was later reported that the patient had made a normal recovery.

"Patience, Madam. Mrs. Remington's poodles psychological disturbance has priority over your suspected rumbling appendix."

Daily Express, 28 June 1984

In view of growing public concern regarding underfunding and other inadequacies of the NHS at the time, a review was carried out during 1988, which culminated in the publication of a White Paper in January 1989 recommending changes.

"Whatever they put in their new Secret White paper it will still include our usual two-hour wait."

Daily Express, 31 January 1989

Grandma and the Law

Two days earlier, the House of Lords had debated the Second Reading of the Street Offences Bill, which closely followed the recommendations of the Wolfenden Committee on Homosexual Offences and Prostitution. In the debate, one member had made several references to Curzon Street.

"Vera, why you have to ask a man the way in Curzon-street I shall never know."

Daily Express, 7 May 1959

In 1962 it became an offence in the UK for any person to drive, attempt to drive or be in charge of, a motor vehicle if their "ability to drive properly was for the time being impaired". No legal drink driving limit was set until 1966, with a breathalyser test coming into force in 1967. However, in this case, the policeman was relying upon legislation under the Penalties for Drunkenness Act, 1962, which came into force earlier that year, to pin a charge upon Grandma.

"Right. You've convinced me you can walk a straight line for a mile – now come back to the station while I charge you."

Daily Express, 21 December 1962

When King Paul and Queen Frederika of Greece arrived for a state visit to London, over 5,000 police were on duty to cope with violent demonstrations on behalf of political prisoners in Greece. It seems that Grandma supported a wide range of good causes.

"Nice work, lads – ninety-four demonstrators, one King, H.R.H., three bus conductors..."

Daily Express, 11 July 1963

A member of the Metropolitan Police Force was answering questions about violent crime in London during the previous week. Asked what advice he would give to members of the public who saw a gunman carrying out a raid, he replied, "It depends entirely on how you are placed in the situation but if you can have a go, have a go". It is doubtful that Grandma had properly considered the situation.

"Git off you old fool! I was only asking him the time."

Sunday Express, 3 January 1965

"This Family Court charges you with unlawfully swigging Grandma's stout through a straw."

Daily Express, 26 August 1965

The day before it had been discovered that a prisoner, described as dangerous, had, on occasions, left working parries outside Dartmoor Prison to ride four miles, on bareback ponies, to a nearby pub. The farmer who lent him the ponies said that he seemed harmless and, over the months, had got to know him well.

"We can't go round thinking everybody riding a horse has escaped from Dartmoor in disguise, Madam."

Daily Express, 20 December 1966

120 There was a great deal of national debate at this time about the dangers of drug taking with the production, in early 1968, of a report prepared by the Hallucinogens Sub-Committee of the Advisory Committee of Drug Dependence, for the Home Office.

"We had an anonymous phone call at the Yard informing us that this lady had been hoarding hemp."

Daily Express, 5 March 1968

This cartoon appeared two days before the 1968 US presidential election. The election featured the strongest third party effort since the 1912 presidential election, by former Alabama Governor, George Wallace. He was a strong advocate for racial segregation in American public schools which, no doubt, was the reason for Grandma's planned "march".

"Grandma, someone's tipped 'em off about your anti-Wallace march to Grosvenor Square"

Sunday Express, 3 November 1968

"Over 21!"

Daily Express, 27 May 1971

This was a period of severe drought with almost no rainfall in the whole country. For more than a month, temperatures were above 27°C (80°F) and often reached 32°C (90°F). A hosepipe ban and other measures to conserve water were introduced with standpipes being used in some areas.

"Think very carefully, sonny – are you absolutely sure that was the man you saw using a hose on his window box?"

Sunday Express, 11 April 1976

The Fencing Act, 1978 set out the rights and responsibilities relating to fences between neighbouring properties. The Act noted that "this was an area that can cause huge friction between neighbours" and that a fence might be needed to serve several purposes – privacy, protection from wind and weather, and also "to keep animals in or out".

"The Spy Computer Service says that on December 7, at 1750 and 20 seconds precisely, this lady did throw a cabbage at her neighbour's poodle who was trespassing upon her lawn. How the devil did this get to the Crown Court?"

Daily Express, 7 December 1978

Severe weather conditions were experienced in the UK at this time with the greatest disruption occurring on the 8th and 9th of January. Heavy snow with a gale force easterly wind produced one of the worst blizzards of the century across southern England, the Midlands, Wales and Ireland. Throughout the period of the snowfall, which lasted over 36 hours, temperatures were between -2 and -4°C (28 and 25°F).

"Before you start – do you mind getting off my skis?"

Daily Express, 12 January 1982

An unusual occurrence – Grandma trying to be friendly.

"You say the lady kissed your head under the mistletoe thereby causing you sexual harassment?"

Daily Express, 21 December 1982

Grandma the Royalist and Political Activist

At this time, there was considerable national discussion about hanging, with the Death Penalty (Abolition) Bill being debated in the House of Lords a week after this cartoon appeared. Nine years later, the Murder (Abolition of Death Penalty) Act, 1965 finally abolished the death penalty for murder in Great Britain (the death penalty for murder survived in Northern Ireland until 1973). The Act replaced the death penalty with a mandatory sentence of imprisonment for life.

"My Grandma says hang everybody."

Daily Express, 3 July 1956

"I've run her round the shops, called on her sister Ivy, dropped her off for an hour's bingo – and I still bet the old faggot votes the other way."

During this period, the leadership election for the Conservative Party was being held to find a successor to Sir Alec Douglas-Home. Edward Heath (Shadow Chancellor), Reginald Maudling (Shadow Foreign Secretary) and Enoch Powell (Shadow Transport Minister) all stood with Heath being elected. Other names considered as possible contenders included Quintin Hogg. Grandma, obviously, had made her views known.

"It was a nice party until someone asked Grandma 'What about Quintin Hogg?'"

Sunday Express, 25 July 1965

The Trades Union Congress conference was being held at Blackpool. Frank Cousins, General Secretary of the then biggest Union, Transport and General Workers, and MP for Nuneaton, put an emergency resolution to the conference regarding the Government's Prices and Incomes Bill and was quoted as saying that he was "frustrated by political influences".

"Anybody taking the minutes of this top-level conference?"

Daily Express, 8 September 1966

Due to fog, Mr. Kosygin's plane had to be diverted from Gatwick to Heathrow. Grandma was not the only one caught out. The plane had to circle around London for a while to give the Prime Minister, Harold Wilson, time to get from Gatwick to Heathrow to welcome the visitor. It's odd that an ardent supporter of royalty like Grandma should wish to give the Soviet Premier such a warm welcome – Or is it? – It is, after all, Grandma.

"It won't be Mr. Kosygin who'll take the can back because Grandma waited for him at the wrong airport."

Daily Express, 7 February 1967

"Grandma, you must let Vera vote for whom she chooses."

Daily Express, 18 June 1970

This cartoon shows Chancellor of the Exchequer, Anthony Barber, holding up the Budget Box for his first budget. In it, he proposed to replace Purchase Tax and Selective Employment Tax with Value Added Tax, and also relaxed exchange controls; both being prerequisites to membership of the European Economic Community. Maybe Grandma's anger is in response to the latter proposals.

"Hold tight, sir."

Daily Express, 30 March 1971

"That's one large Martini down the drain – she said 'Thanks comrade.'"

Sunday Express, 24 February 1974

"The last one put his coat down and bought me two gins and tonics."

Sunday Express, 6 October 1974

136 The occasion was the Queens 50th birthday. It refers back to the cartoon Giles prepared for the menu cover of the Queen's and Prince Philip's Silver Wedding Anniversary dinner, organised by Prince Charles and Princess Anne, which featured Grandma delivering her present of six spoons, bearing the initials "BR", to Buckingham Palace (see cartoon on page 7).

"Good morning, Madam, aren't we the lady that got done for sending Her Majesty six British Railway spoons for her silver Wedding?"

Daily Express, 20 April 1976

Grandma preparing for the wedding of Prince Charles, Prince of Wales and Lady Diana Spencer three days later.

"You'll have to take it off Grandma – Butch doesn't like it!"

Sunday Express, 26 July 1981

Charles and Diana decided to marry at St Paul's Cathedral instead of Westminster Abbey, the traditional location for royal weddings, because St Paul's had more seating and allowed a longer procession through the streets of London. They obviously forgot to tell Grandma.

"I told her it's at St. Paul's but she says they always have 'em here."

Daily Express, 29 July 1981

Rather like the six BR spoons for the Queen's Silver Wedding Anniversary, this was another dubious present to members of the Royal family – this time for the wedding of Charles and Diana. Unsurprisingly, it took four Guardsmen and two Beefeaters to control Grandma.

"Playing up 'ell because she couldn't find her woolly egg warmer on show"

Daily Express, 6 August 1981

Grandma in political mode.

"10 Downing Street say they will give Grandma a knighthood if she will lay off politics for five minutes so we can have a nap."

Sunday Express, 9 February 1986

"Another reason we hope you won't be sitting here tomorrow – your embrocation is upsetting our tracker dogs."

Daily Express, 22 July 1986

It is not recorded how often Grandma popped in for a "cuppa" and a chat about the state of the nation with the Prime Minister.

"Thank you so much for calling and advising me on the changes I must make in 1987. Now hop it."

Daily Express, 30 December 1986

This shows that Grandma sometimes had a rather unfocussed approach to politics.

"If the Honourable member of the public directed her political expressions to one party only it would help the peace."

Sunday Express, 22 February 1987

This was the 88th birthday of Queen Elizabeth, the Queen Mother, who, at that time, lived at Clarence House. Presumably Grandma considered that two elderly great-grandmothers could probably spend an enjoyable evening together, over a drink, talking about old times.

"Can her Majesty slip out for a quick half of bitter for her birthday?"

Daily Express, 4 August 1988

It had been reported that the Chancellor of the Exchequer, Nigel Lawson, was considering scrapping pensioners' rights to some welfare benefits including free medical prescriptions and the £10 Christmas bonus. Grandma obviously had strong opinions on this, even if she was targeting the wrong person.

"You've chained yourself to the wrong railings, duckie – the Chancellor lives next door."

Daily Express, 8 November 1988

Soviet President Mikhail S. Gorbachev arrived at Heathrow airport for a short 40-hour visit including discussions with Prime Minister, Margaret Thatcher, which would "mix hard talk on human rights with traditional British pageantry". Grandma's appearance was probably designed to help the debate along.

"You've missed him. If you hurry you might catch him before he leaves Downing Street."

Daily Express, 6 April 1989

Grandma and Anger Management

This is at the Epsom Derby where French horse, "Seabird", galloped to a 2-length victory. Grandma's horse must have lost and she was taking out her anger at losing on Pat Glennon, Seabird's Australian jockey, which seems a little unfair.

"She always was a poor loser."

Daily Express, 3 June 1965

Grandma losing control at Cowes Week.

"When I said she's a bit wide across the beam I didn't mean you, you old faggot."

Sunday Express, 1 August 1965

A Scots girl, aged 21, had lost her job in an estate agents office in Folkestone because her accent was too strong. The office manager explained "She speaks very broadly and I, my staff and clients could not always understand her".

"You don't need an interpreter to translate Grandma's comments. Her wee Grandpa came from bonnie Dundee."

Daily Express, 8 November 1966

It had just been announced that a company specialising in cut-price car insurance had become insolvent and rumours that the Board of Trade was investigating a number of other similar companies at the same time had been confirmed.

"Madam, I assure you there's no danger of my company folding and your 7d. a week for the last sixty years going up the spout."

Daily Express, 23 January 1967

A Voluntary Euthanasia Bill was being discussed in the House of Lords and, just previously, the Voluntary Euthanasia Society had been established.

"Put the doctor down, Grandma. He's come about Ernie's measles, not to bump you off"

Daily Express, 2 May 1969

152   This was during the Three-Day Week when measures were introduced to conserve electricity, and television companies were required to cease broadcasting at 10.30 pm. The book relates to George Orwell's *1984* which predicted a world where "Big Brother is watching you". Grandma obviously did not completely agree with the views expressed in that evening's Party Political Broadcast.

"That's Grandma's SOS for the day – good night party political broadcast."

Daily Express, 24 January 1974

"As usual, the one who's doing the most hollering is the one who's never put a penny in the TV licence box in her life."

Daily Express, 31 January 1975

Probably Giles was referring to the normal pre-Christmas crush on the London underground when Grandma's short temper would be sorely tested.

"Hold it, man – we can't go around punching happy shoppers just because they poked their Christmas tree in your eye."

Daily Express, 11 December 1979

This was a period when rioting broke out in many towns and cities around England. It appears that Grandma did not approve of other people's bad behaviour.

"Typical ain't it? When you really need a copper you can never find one."

Sunday Express, 12 July 1981

156 In November, 1984, the Government offered BT shares to the public. The day before this cartoon appeared, the Minister of State for Industry and Information Technology announced in the House of Commons – "We received more than 2 million applications for the 1,000 million shares available. The Government has decided to give priority to smaller applications, and all applications for 200 and 400 shares are therefore being met in full. Applicants for 800 and 1,200 shares will receive 500 and 600 shares respectively. Applicants for higher numbers up to a maximum of 100,000 shares will receive 800 shares. No allocation will be made to applicants for over 100,000 shares". Perhaps we should add "greed" to Grandma's many other shortcomings!

"Whoa there! We warned you if you went for over 100,000 Telecom shares you might end up with none!"

Daily Express, 4 December 1984

It should not come as a great surprise that she had threatened football referees in the past.

"Threatening football referees is one thing – slapping Flower Show judges because you didn't get a Highly Commended is another!"

Daily Express, 21 May 1985

The previous day, a builder was sentenced to two and a half years imprisonment for "unlawful wounding" – he had shot an intruder in the legs. It was stated that he had taken the law into his own hands, having had numerous raids on his country cottage. He had reported ten cases of theft and damage, costing around a total of £20,000, and felt that the police had taken no action. The defending solicitor had argued that "he had acted within his rights to guard his possessions, challenge trespassers and see offenders off his land". The young man must have read the solicitor's statement.

"Watch it! I can get you 2½ years inside if you hit me just because I nicked your pension book."

Sunday Express, 15 November 1987